INFOGRAPHICS

THE ENCYCLOPEDIA
OF
MODERN
TRANSPORT

TODAY'S VEHICLES IN FACTS AND FIGURES

BY SVIATOSLAV YEZHELYI
ILLUSTRATED BY NATALIA BOLDYRIEVA

PUBLISHING HOUSE
RANOK

The Encyclopedia of Modern Transport
Today's Vehicles in Facts and Figures
Series: Infographics for Kids

First published in 2018 by "Encyclopedias"
Redesigned for global publishing by Luda Werdin in 2019.
Luda Werdin is the official representative of Publishing House Ranok Limited authorized to act on its behalf.

ISBN: 978-617-09-5786-3

Publishing House Ranok Limited
135-27 Kibalchicha street, Kharkiv, Ukraine, 61071
"Encyclopedias" is a division of Publishing House Ranok Limited
For more information, contact "Encyclopedias",
21a Kosmichna street, Entrance 1, Floor 6,
Kharkiv, Ukraine, 61145
Email: office@ranok.com.ua
Edited by Iryna Petrenko
Book design by Natalia Boldyrieva

CONTENTS

ELECTRIC CARS

ELECTRIC CAR

This convenient, noiseless, and environmentally friendly means of transport is becoming more and more popular nowadays. The electric car is moved not by a gas combustion engine but by an electric motor that receives power from a rechargeable battery.

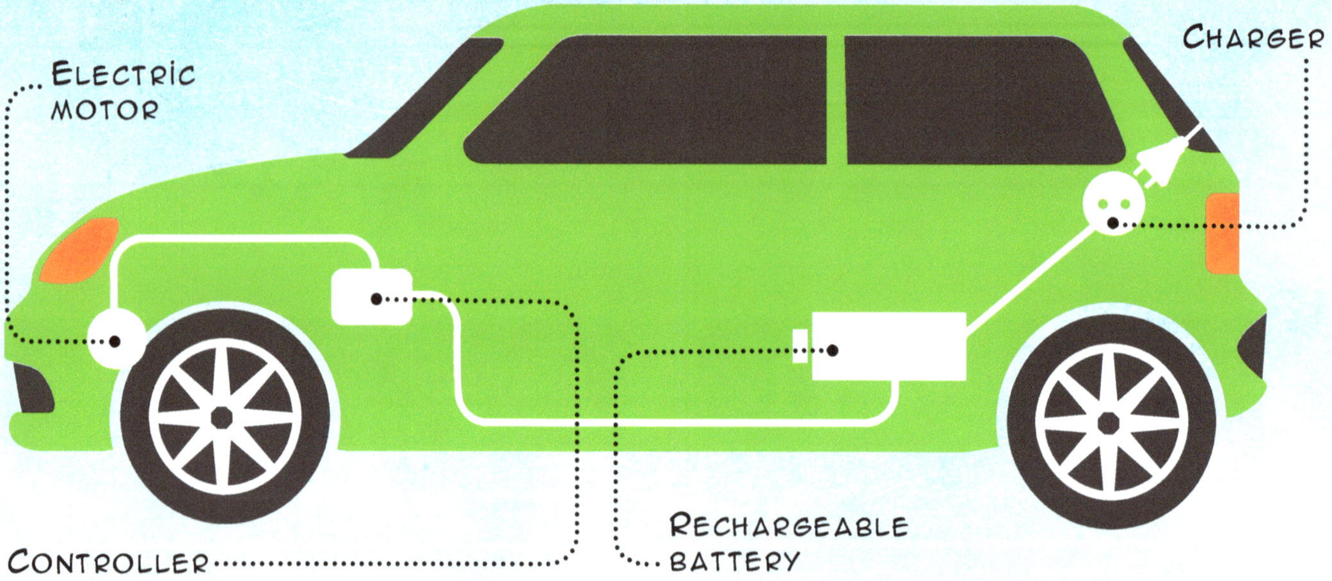

1834

An academician Boris Jacobi assembles the first electric motor in the world.

1838

Scottish Robert Davidson designs a car with the electric motor getting its power supply from huge tanks filled with sulfuric acid.

1895

Charles Jeantaud designs a two-seated electric car which can accelerate to a speed of 40 mph.

1888

In the US, a three-wheel vehicle is equipped with an electric motor.

1881

A French Charles Jeantaud equips a four-wheel cart with an electric motor.

1899

A Belgian Camille Jenatzy builds a legendary rocket-shaped vehicle "La Jamais Contente".

1901

Fred White and Walter Baker create an electric car which can run 18.75 mph for as far as 50 miles.

1996

General Motors Company announces the start of full-scale electric car production.

1907

Detroit Electric Company starts manufacturing and selling electric cars.

1902

The Studebaker brothers start producing custom-made electric cars.

2008

Tesla Motors Company launches the Tesla Roadster sports car production.

2010–2013

World records in speed and distance for modern electric cars are set.

2017

One of the fastest gas engine cars — the Bugatti Veyron — loses the race to the Rimac Concept One electric car.

ELECTRIC CARS

MORE THAN 1 000 000 ELECTRIC CARS HAVE BEEN SOLD IN THE WORLD

SILENT MOVEMENT

The first electric car to speed up to 62.5 mph was the "La Jamais Contente" electric car.

SOME ELECTRIC CARS ARE EQUIPPED WITH AN AUTOPILOT

THE PRINCIPLE OF ELECTRIC MOTOR OPERATION

The driving element of the electric car is an electric motor.
The principle of its operation is the same as that of a radio-controlled toy car.
The simplest motor consists of a magnet and a wire. If a wire loop, through which electric current is running, is placed between the north and the south poles of the magnet, the magnetic field begins to repel the wire and the loop starts rotating. This principle is used in all kinds of electric motors.

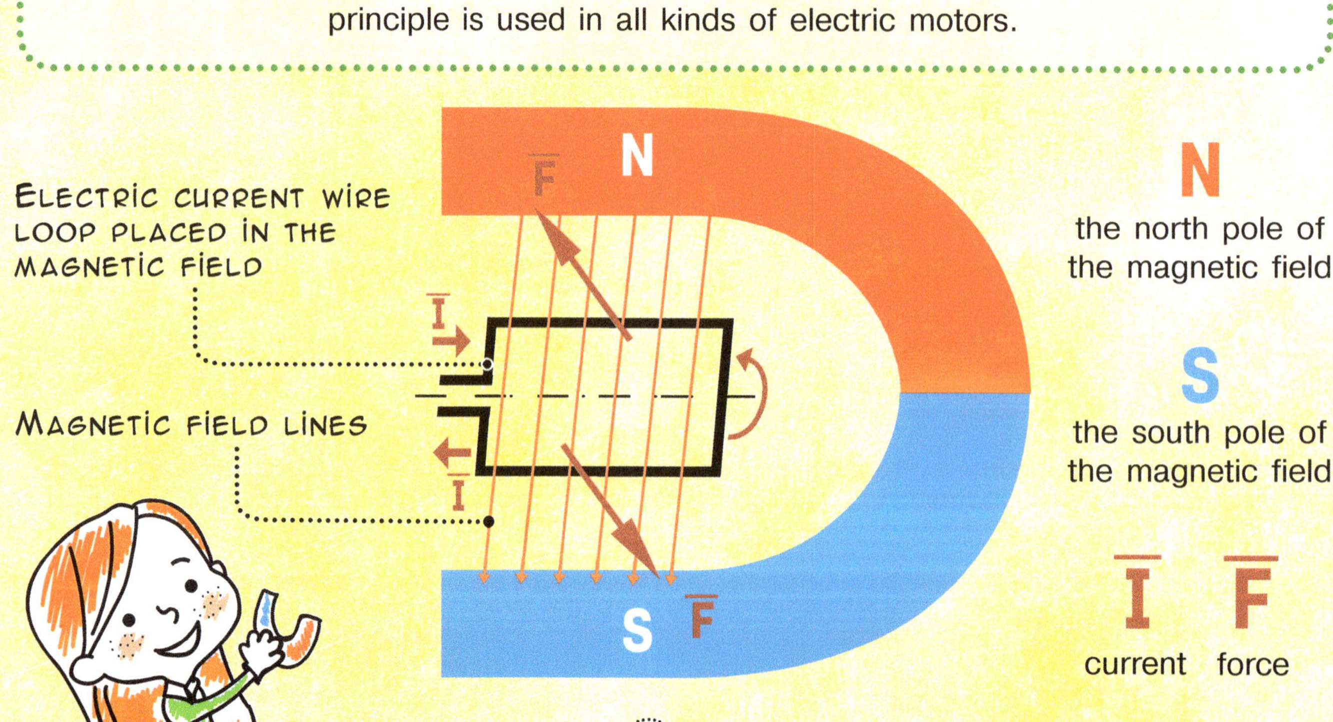

FOR CLEAN FUTURE!

The electric car is an environmentally friendly means of transport. Its motor is supplied with power by rechargeable batteries. That is why the environment is not polluted by a large amount of harmful exhaust gases. Every year, the popularity of electric cars increases. In the future, this tendency will help to solve the problem of atmospheric gas pollution.

MAGNETOPLANES

THE MAGLEV TRAIN

The super high-speed maglev train is moved by the force of an artificial magnetic field. This kind of transport glides in the air above an iron band without touching it. The maglev movement is based on the principle of magnetic levitation.

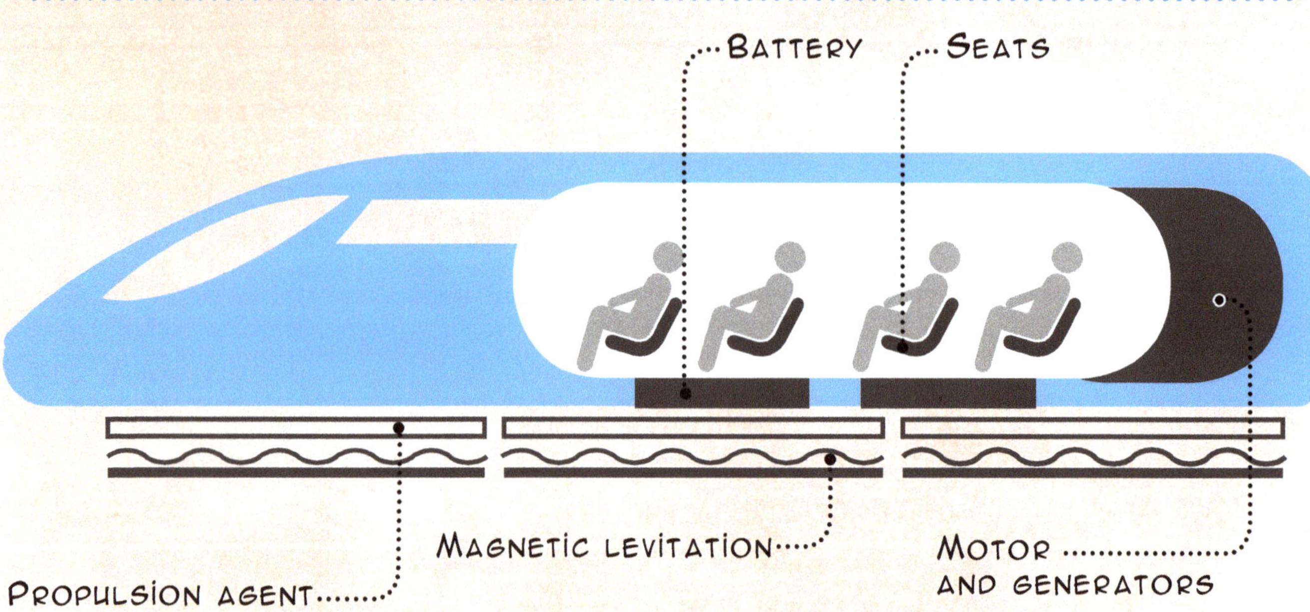

ELECTRIC MAGNETS ON THE ROAD LIFT THE WAGON

ELECTRIC MAGNETS UNDER THE WAGON LIFT IT

PERMANENT MAGNETS LIFT THE WAGON ABOVE THE COILS

1909

An American scientist Robert Goddard introduces the theory of train magnetic levitation.

1913

Boris Weinberg carries out experiments on moving a capsule in a tube under the influence of the magnetic field.

1971

Germany launches the first passenger wagon "Transrapid-02".

1934

A German engineer Hermann Kemper invents magnetic suspension.

1984

The first commercial maglev appears in England.

1999

An American engineer Daryl Oster patents the technology of evacuated tube transport.

2005

Japan takes the "Linimo" maglev train line into operation.

2004

The airport of Shanghai launches a maglev line with a German "Transrapid" train.

2012

Elon Musk suggests the project of vacuum Hyperloop maglev train on the magnetic cushion.

2016

The first tests for Hyperloop-One engine are carried out.

MAGNETOPLANES

PNEUMATIC TUBE

The idea of vacuum transport is based on the pneumatic tube. About 100 years ago in New York, encapsulated letters were sent via rarefied air tubes.

625 mph

Due to no friction between the train and the road, a maglev can develop the speed of over 625 mph.

IN VACUUM TUBES, THE TRAIN SPEED CAN BE SEVERAL TIMES HIGHER THAN THE SPEED OF SOUND

MAGNETIC LEVITATION

Magnets, facing each other with similar poles, repel, and with different poles — attract each other. These properties are used for maglev trains movement and their levitation above the rails.

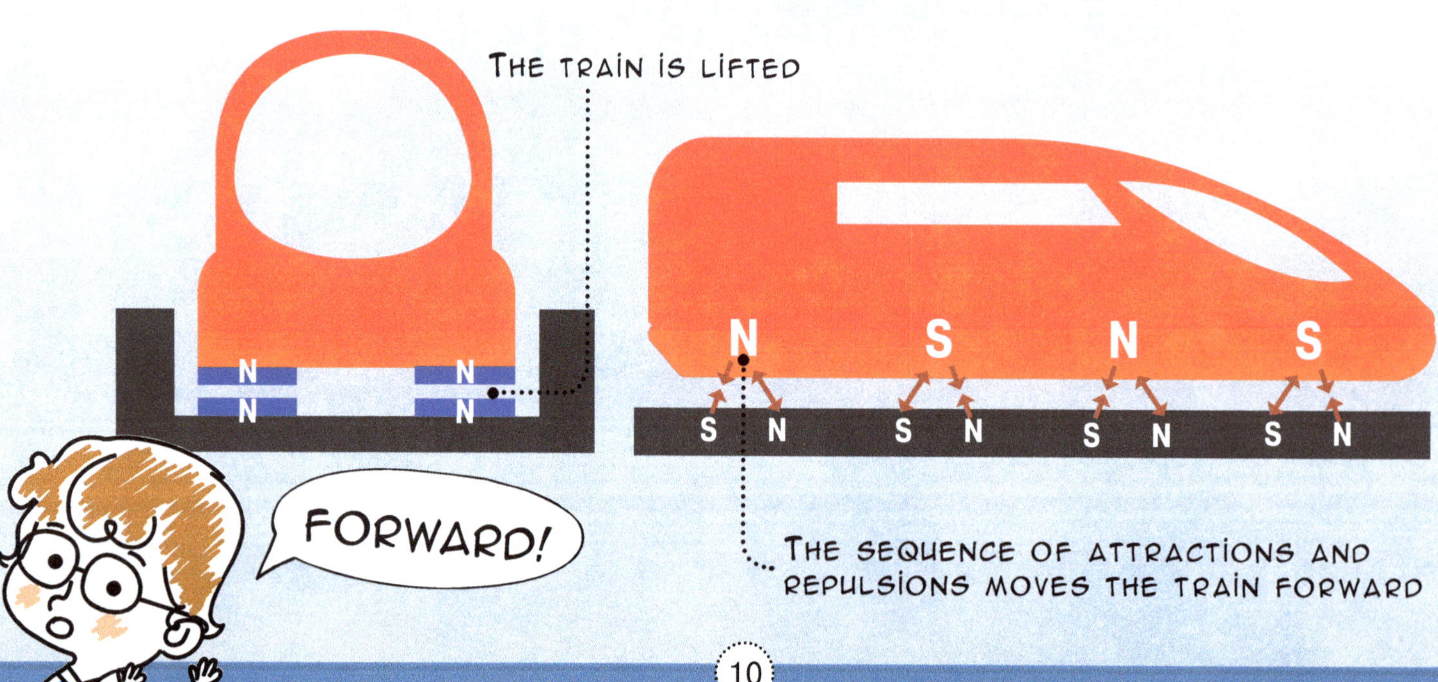

THE FASTEST MAGNETOPLANES

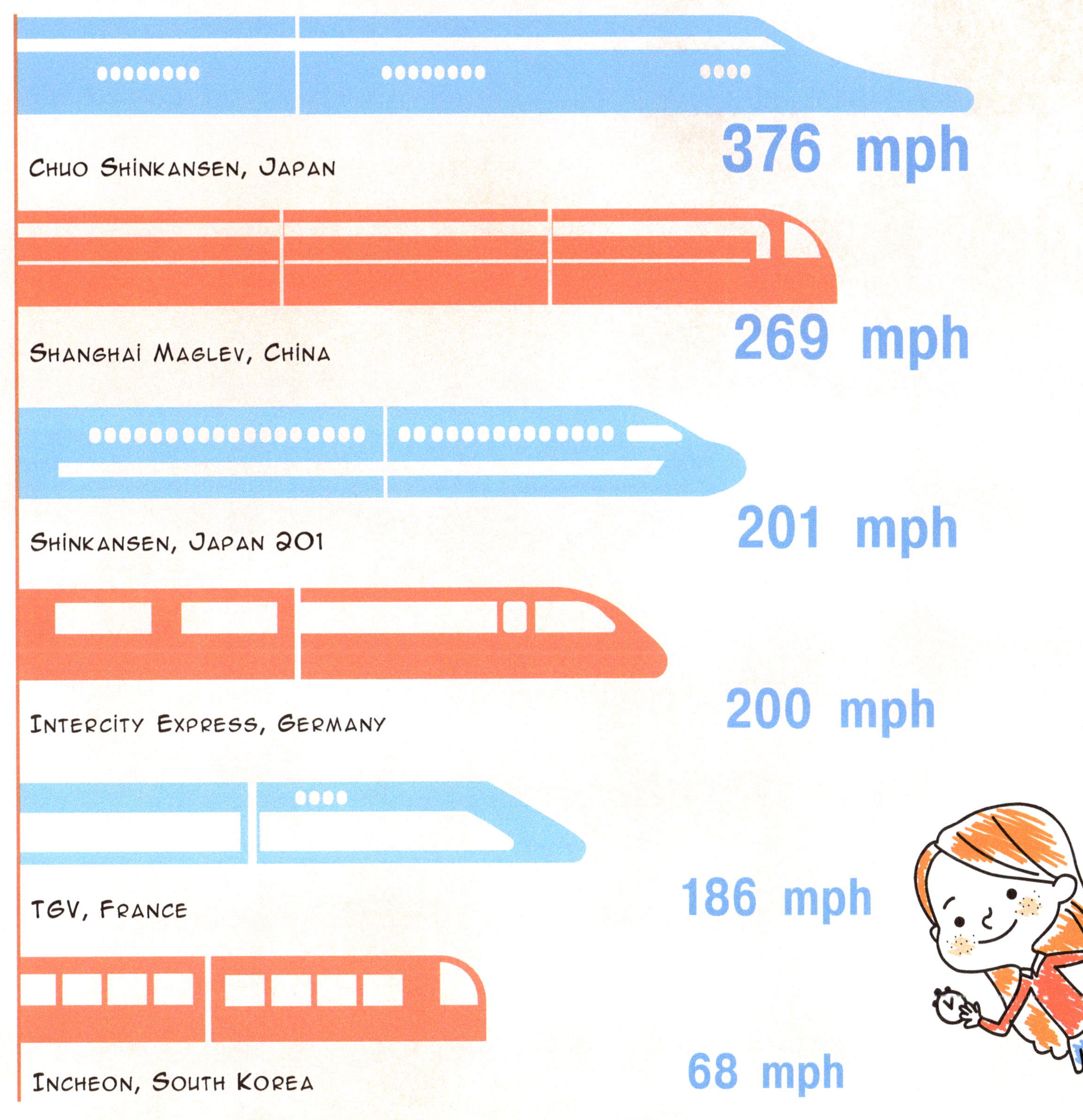

A maglev train on the magnetic cushion is the fastest and most energy efficient means of transport. By 2049, people will be able to use maglevs to cover 1000 miles just in a matter of hours.

UNMANNED AIRCRAFT

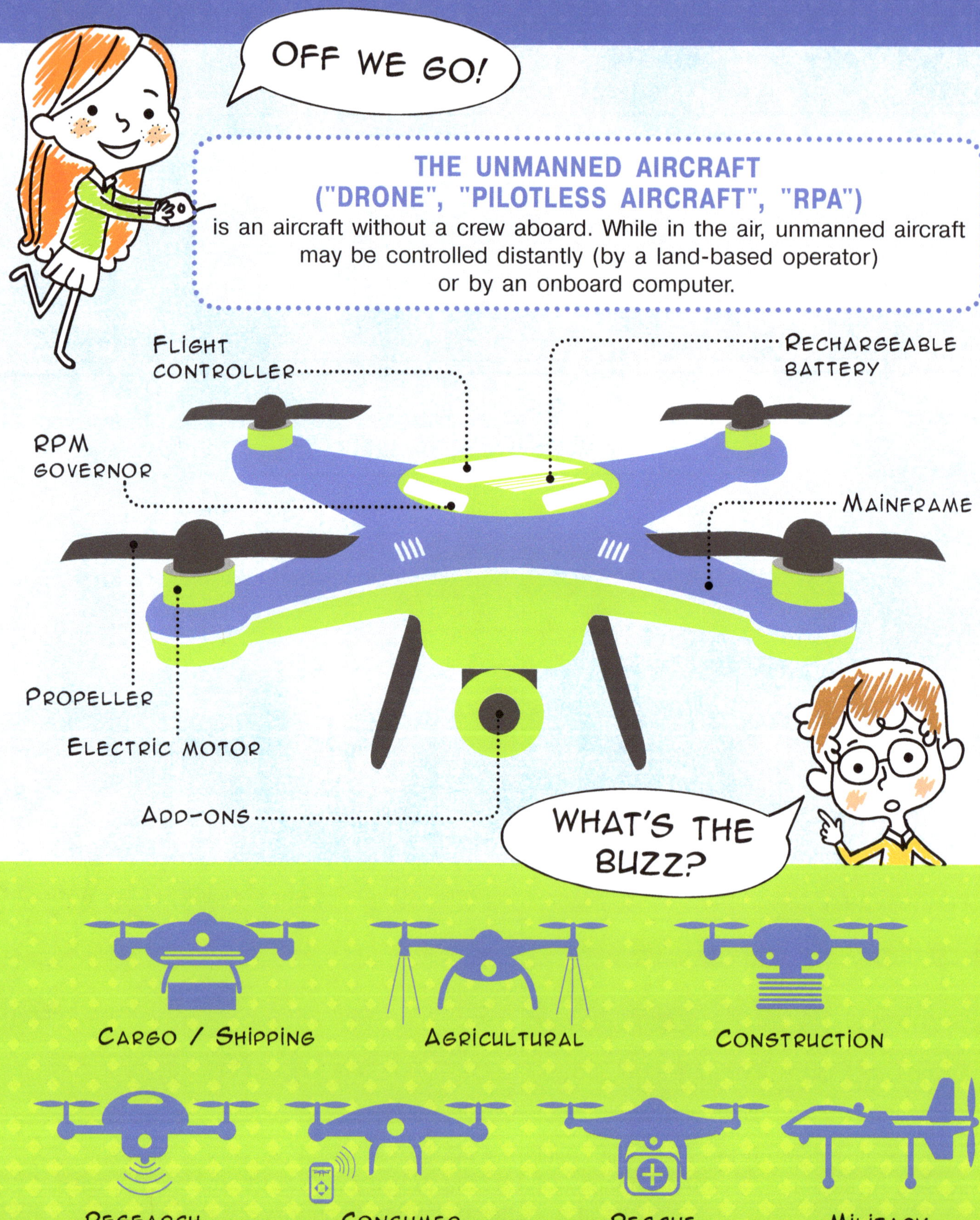

1898 — Nikola Tesla designs a miniature radio controlled boat.

1909 — Charles Kettering invents a clockwork aircraft.

1933 — Great Britain designs the first unmanned aircraft "DH.82B Queen Bee".

1941 — A radio-controlled plane TB-3 "Bomb" is tested successfully.

1942 — The first unmanned bomber "Interstate TDR1" is put into operation in the US.

2000 — A number of commercial unmanned aircrafts appear.

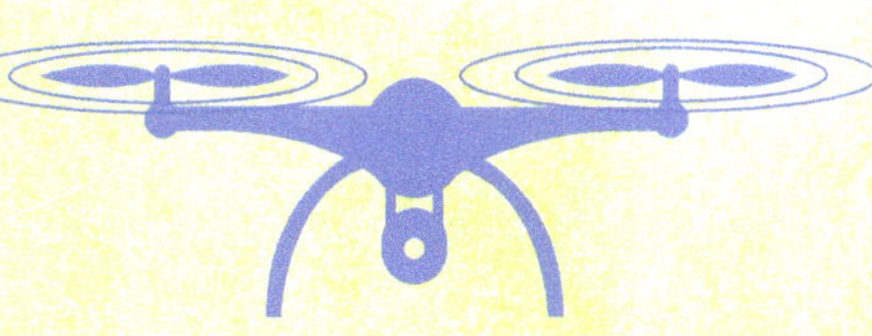

2014 — The US company Amazon uses unmanned aircrafts for shipping goods.

2017 — A new profession — "unmanned aircraft operator" — appears.

UNMANNED AIRCRAFT

An outstanding inventor Leonardo da Vinci investigated air traction which is the basis for unmanned aircraft operation.

DRONES CAN INTERACTIVELY PERFORM ONE TASK AS A GROUP

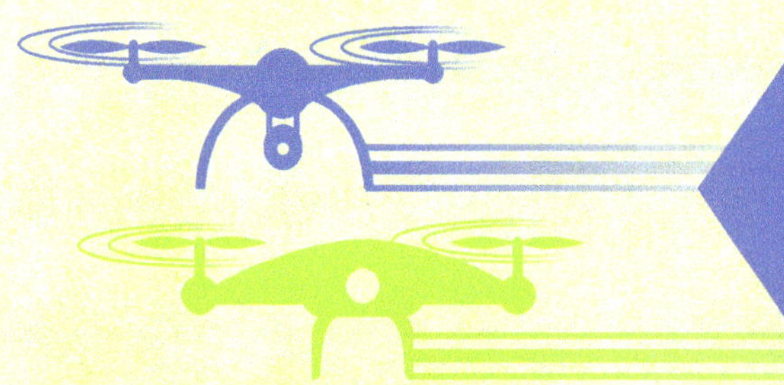

Today, still more popularity is being gained by a new kind of sport — "drone racing" — in which radio controlled aircrafts compete.

WHY DRONES TAKE OFF

Propellers create an air flow which lifts the aircraft and lets it move. When one of four motors works more slowly, the drone tilts towards it. During a turn, two opposite motors work more slowly, and the two others make the drone rotate.

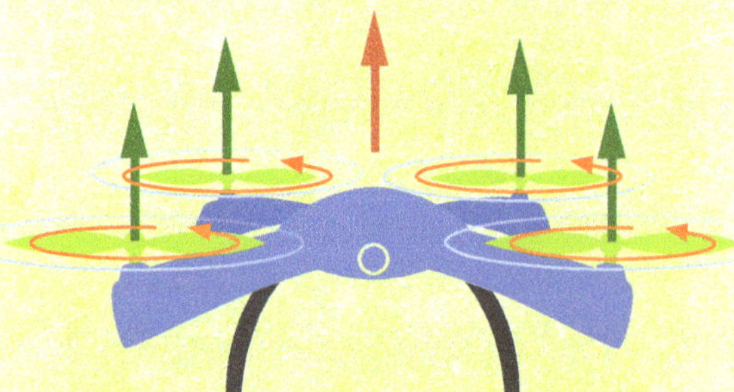

Taking off and pushing down

Turning

Tilting and rotating

AIRSPACE LOAD

TODAY

IN THE NEAREST FUTURE

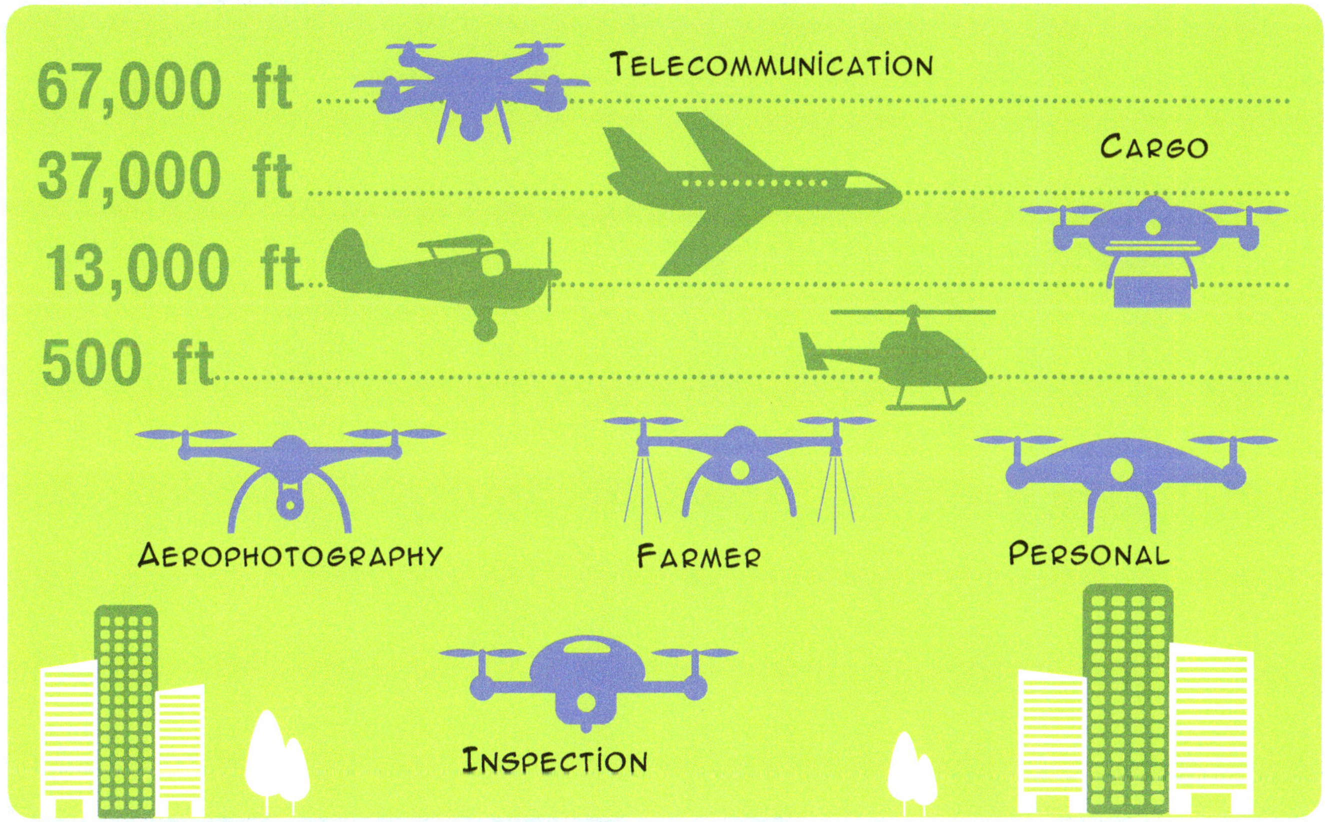

The field of drone use is growing rapidly. Unmanned aircrafts open new ways of research not available before. Drones can deliver cargos to out-of-the-way places, detect natural disasters, monitor public order, carry out photographing and video recording, fertilize fields, and even pick volcanic rock from erupted magma.

Rocket carrier

SPACE TRANSPORT
is used for moving through space. With its help, scientists carry out research expeditions, deliver cargos into orbit or transport people.

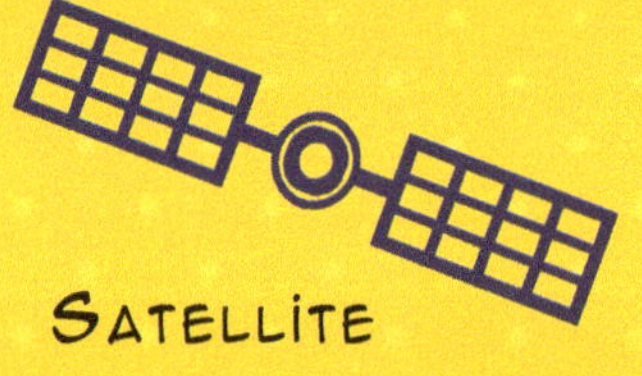

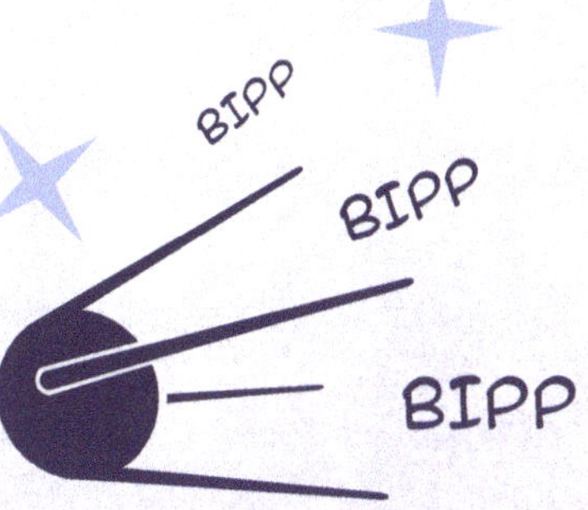

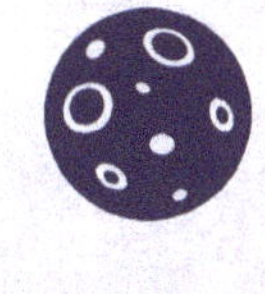

1957
The first artificial satellite is launched under Sergey Korolyov's guidance.

1959
The "Luna-2" interplanetary station reaches the Moon surface for the first time.

1971
The Soviet station "Salyut-1" is placed into orbit.

1969
An American astronaut Neil Armstrong is the first to walk on the Moon surface on the "Apollo-11" spaceship.

1961
Yuri Gagarin is the first man to fly into space on board the Soviet spaceship 'Vostok-1'.

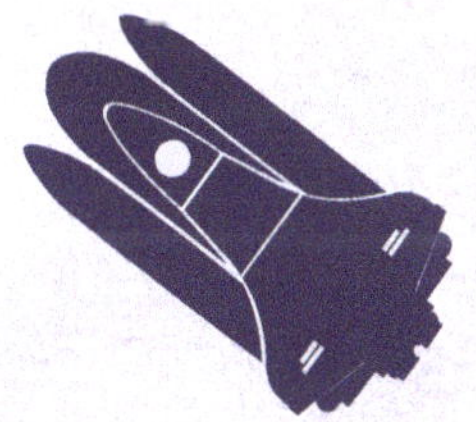

1975
Interplanetary stations "Venera-9" and "Venera-10" land on the surface of Venus.

1981
The first spacecraft "Space Shuttle" is launched.

1998
The permanent ISS with an international crew starts operating.

2018
The SpaceX launches successfully a super heavy "Falcon Heavy" rocket carrier with a Tesla electric car aboard.

2015
The new era of shuttle spacecrafts! The SpaceX "Falcon-9" rocket carrier returns to the platform after the launch.

2004
The first private spaceship "SpaceShipOne" is launched.

IN SPACE

The first solid fuel rocket was invented in Ancient China. A bamboo stick with a mixture of gunpowder and saltpeter inside worked on the same principle as fireworks.

THE LONGEST SPACE FLIGHT HAS BEEN PERFORMED BY THE "VOYAGER" SPACECRAFT

FOR A WHOLE OF 40 YEARS!

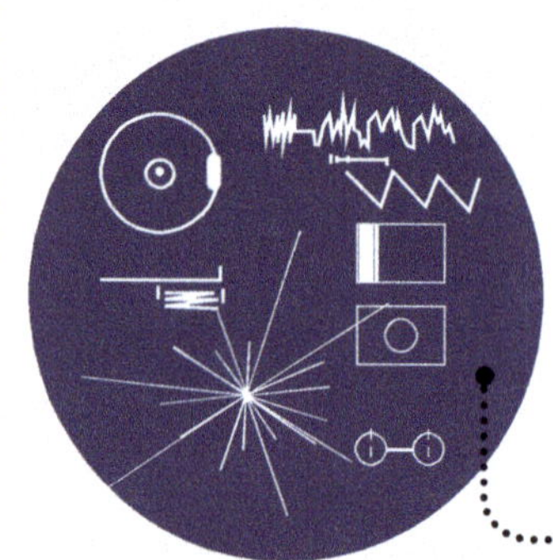

THE LONGEST DISTANCE THAT THE MAN HAS MOVED AWAY FROM THE EARTH IS

237,500 miles

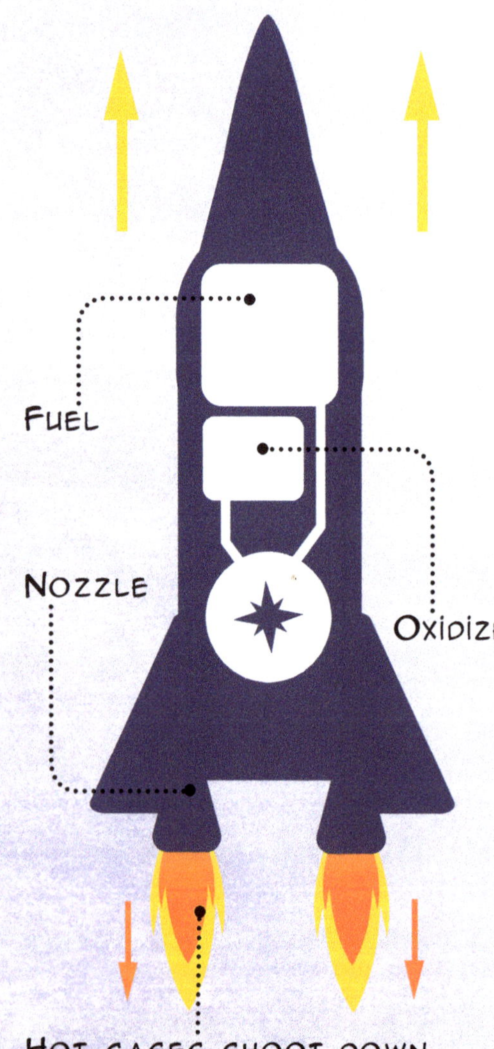

HOW A ROCKET FLIES
A rocket goes up due to powerful fuel combustion. Hot gases go out of the nozzle at a high speed pushing the spacecraft into the opposite direction. A similar effect can be observed when a balloon is let go. The air starts coming out of it, and the balloon flies swiftly.

CIRCUMTERRESTRIAL SPACE DEVICES

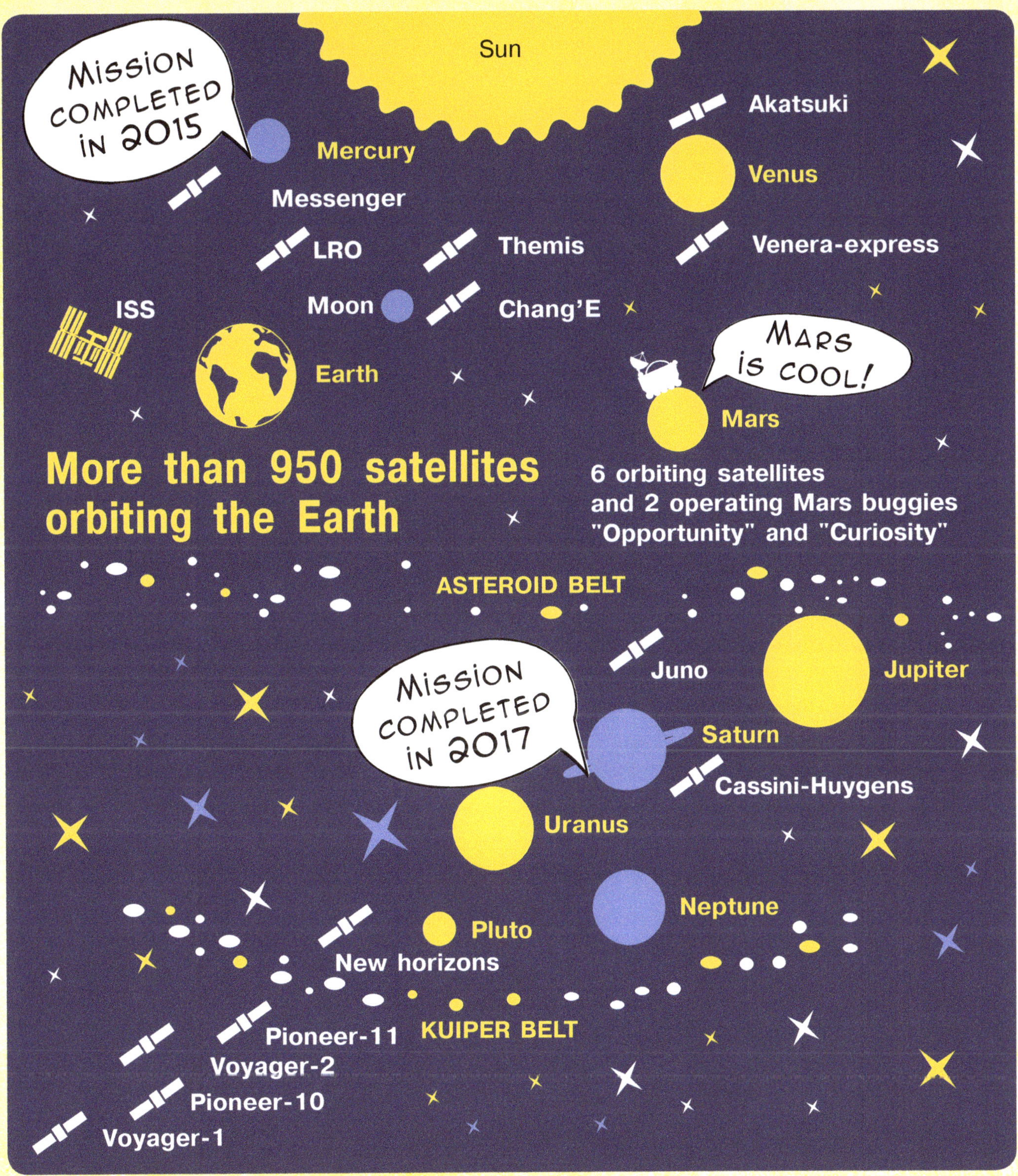

Today, about 1,000 spacecrafts of various intended purposes work in space. Most of them are concentrated around the Earth, the others are in outer space. Every year the number of spacecrafts increases.

GYRO VEHICLES

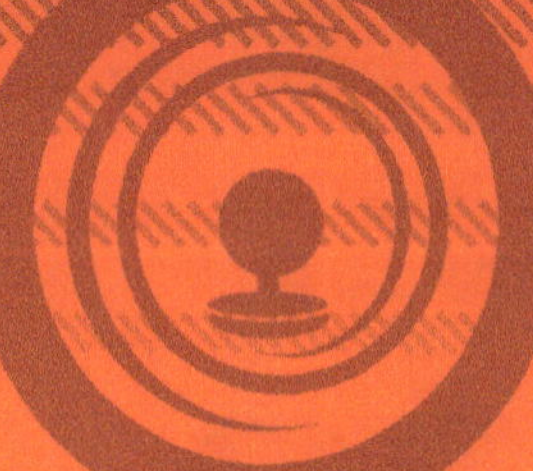

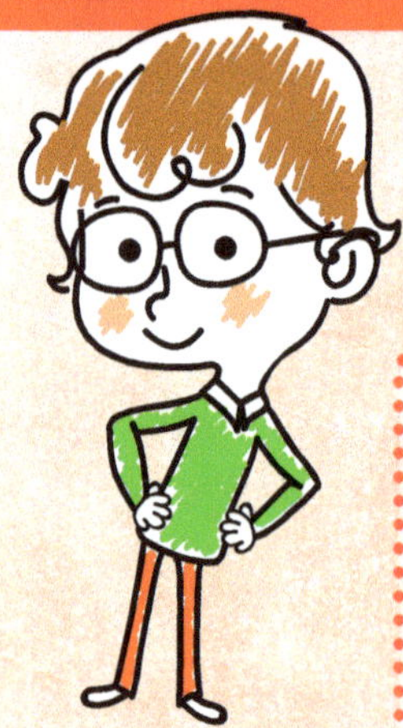

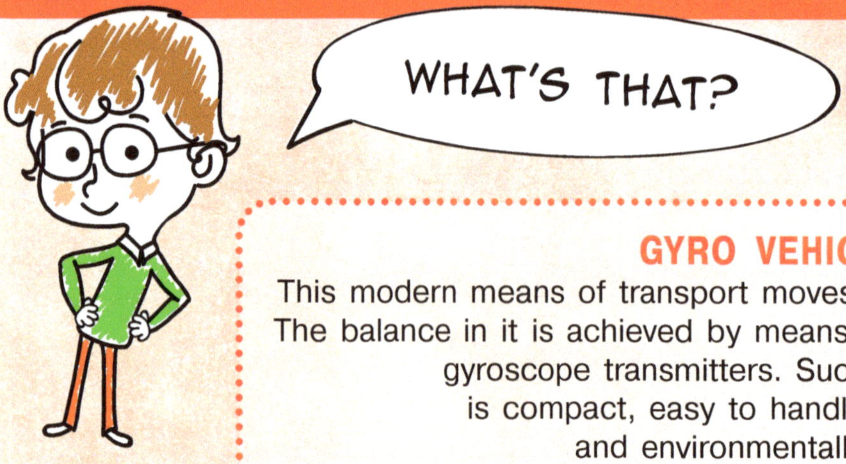

GYRO VEHICLES

This modern means of transport moves due to small electric motors. The balance in it is achieved by means of special balance devices — gyroscope transmitters. Such kind of transport is compact, easy to handle, maneuverable, and environmentally friendly.

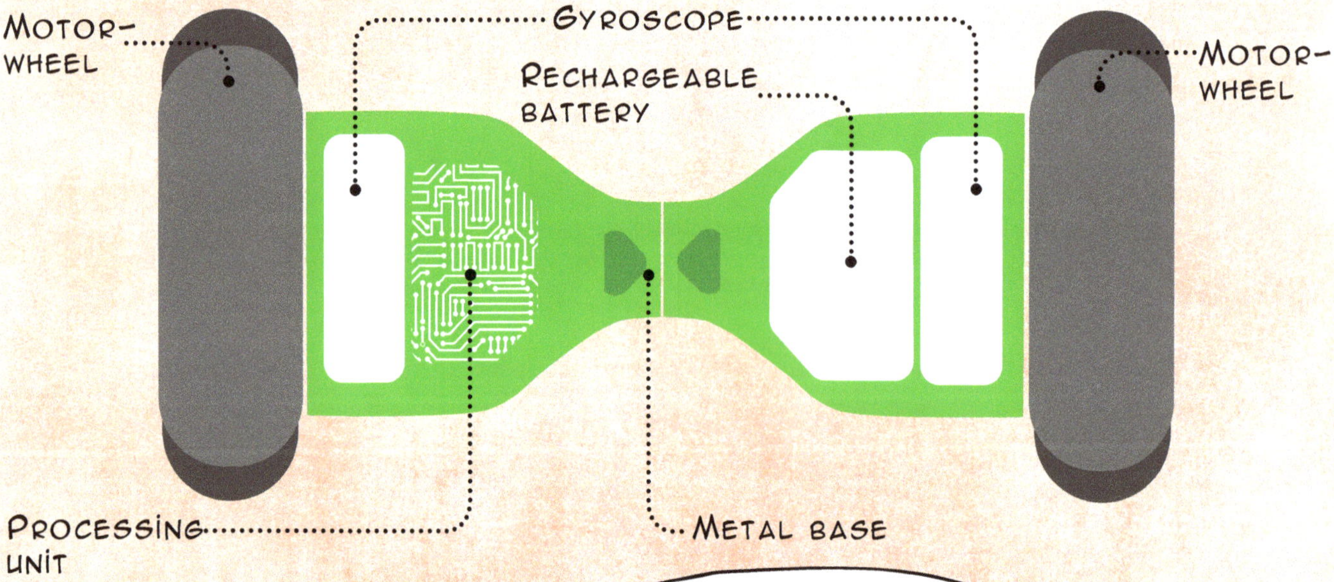

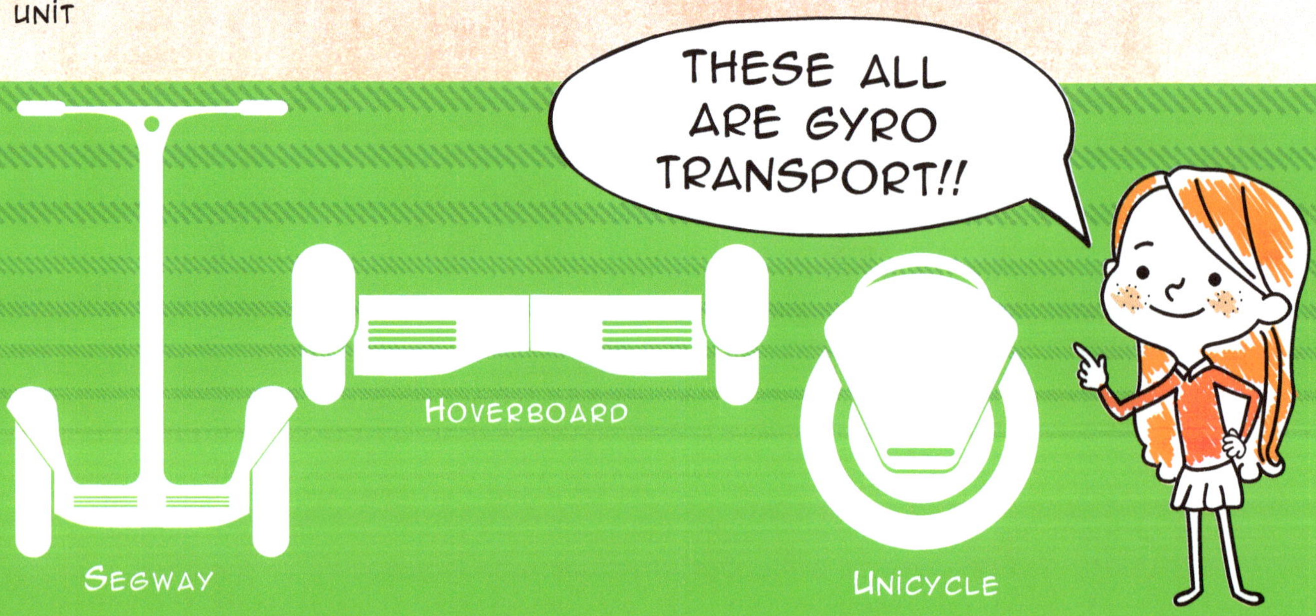

HOVERBOARD

1913

A Russian count Piotr Shilovskyi designs the first gyroscope car in history.

2001

An American inventor Dean Kamen presents the first Segway model to the public.

2002

The 'Segway HT-i167' model overfills the market.

2004

The first hoverboards come into the market.

UNICYCLE

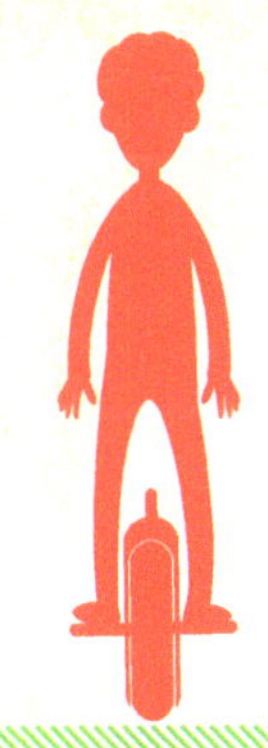

1911

American Tom Coats Clinton presents his invention — the monocycle.

1930

John Archibald Purves designs the 'Dynasphere'.

2006

Kerry McLean makes a monocycle with 225 horsepower.

2009

The Solowheel Company produces the first unicycle with gyroscope balance.

THE SEGWAY CAN GO UP TO

30 mph

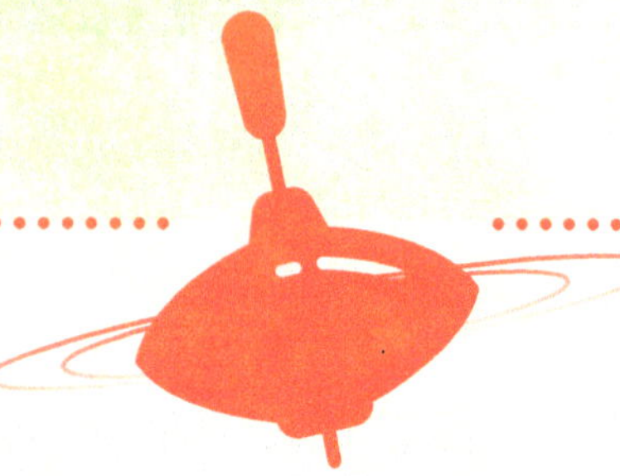

The simplest example of a gyroscope is a spinning top which keeps balancing while rotating on a single pivot.

FANCY MEANS OF TRANSPORT ARE USED BOTH FOR LEISURE AND FOR WORK IN VARIOUS FIELDS

STROLLING IN THE PARK

EXCURSIONS AROUND THE CITY

POLICE PATROL

UNLOADING GOODS

The device platform contains gyroscope sensors. They detect the state the platform is in. The device responds to the change of the person's body position and moves forward or backward respectively.

HOW TO OPERATE A GYRO VEHICLE?

To start moving, you need to lean forward. The bigger the bend, the higher the speed. By leaning backward, you stop moving or move backward. Turning is performed with the help of the handlebar.

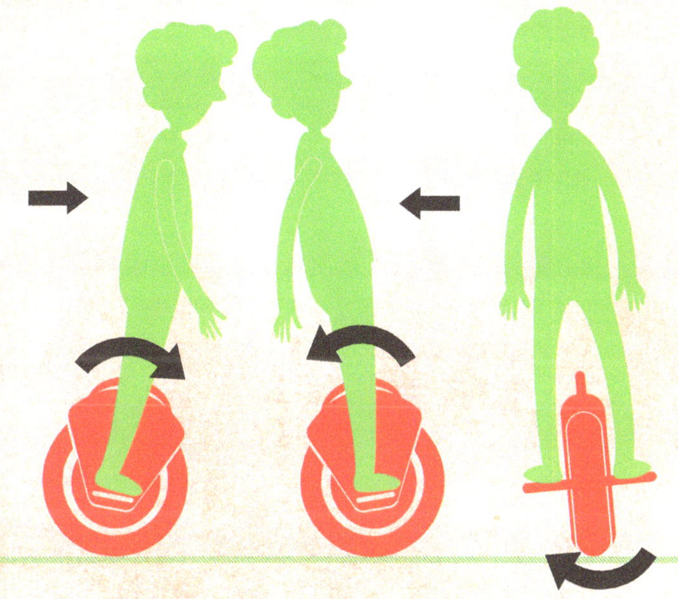

To start moving, you need to lean your body forward, just like with the Segway, and then press your foot against the footboard.
To stop, you need to lean backward and press the heels against the footboard.
To turn, you should press the corresponding side of the footboard.

It's operated exactly as the unicycle.
Yet, when turning right, you need to move your body weight onto the left wheel, and when turning left — onto the right one.

WATER TRANSPORT

RIDE THE WAVE!

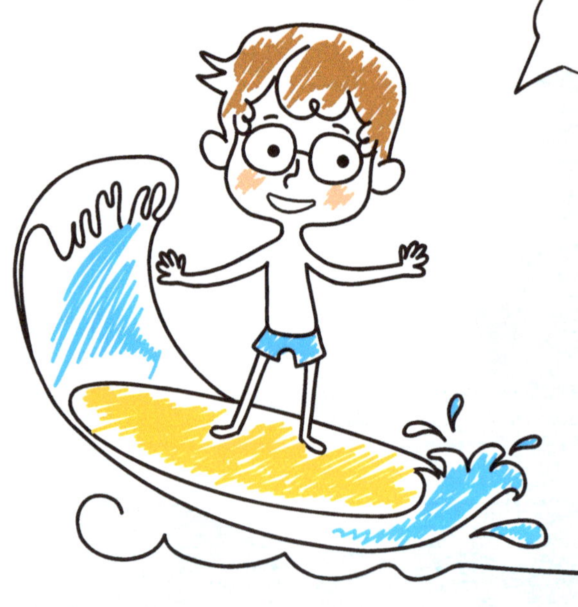

WATER TRANSPORT
moves on or beneath the water surface. Personal water transport is used for scientific investigation of the rivers, seas, and the depths of the ocean. It is also used for entertainment: excursions and doing extreme water sports. Most of the contemporary personal water vessels move with the help of water jet propulsion units.

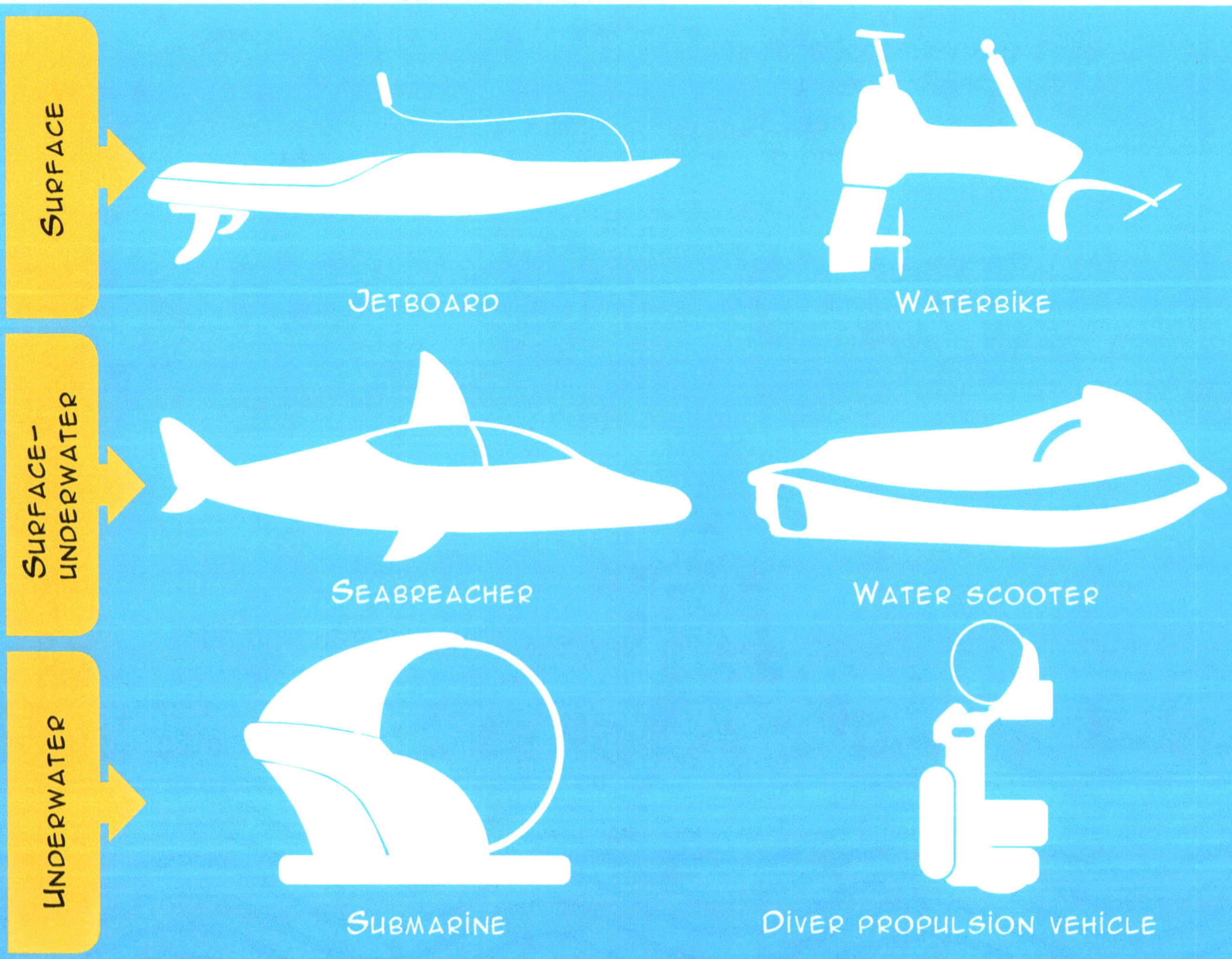
Surface
Jetboard
Waterbike
Surface-underwater
Seabreacher
Water scooter
Underwater
Submarine
Diver propulsion vehicle

1849

Henry Bessemer invents a perfect type of a water-propulsion jet.

1931

The US Navy submarine "USS Nautilus" starts being used for underwater investigations.

1964

Jacques Piccard sets afloat the first tourist submarine "Auguste Piccard".

1965

The first motorized surf board "Jetboard" is created.

2003

The German company Cayago AG starts manufacturing the 'Seabob' DPV.

2006

Rob Innes and Dan Piazza assemble a model of a "Seabreacher" dolphin surface-underwater vessel.

2007

The first entertainment electric underwater scooter "Hydra BOB" is created.

2008

Martin Šula starts the Jet Surf Company producing water propulsion jet surf boards.

2010

Guy Howard-Willis starts working on "Manta 5" hydrofoil bike.

WATER TRANSPORT

The underwater scooter supplies compressed air tanks for passengers to breathe.

The water jet propulsion unit works pretty much the same as that of the moving squid.

STEERING SYSTEMS OF SOME WATERCRAFTS RESEMBLE FISH FINS.

A DOLPHIN-LIKE 'SEABREACHER' WATERCRAFT USES AIR FORCE AIRCRAFT GLASS AS THIS MATERIAL CAN WITHSTAND SIGNIFICANT OVERLOAD.

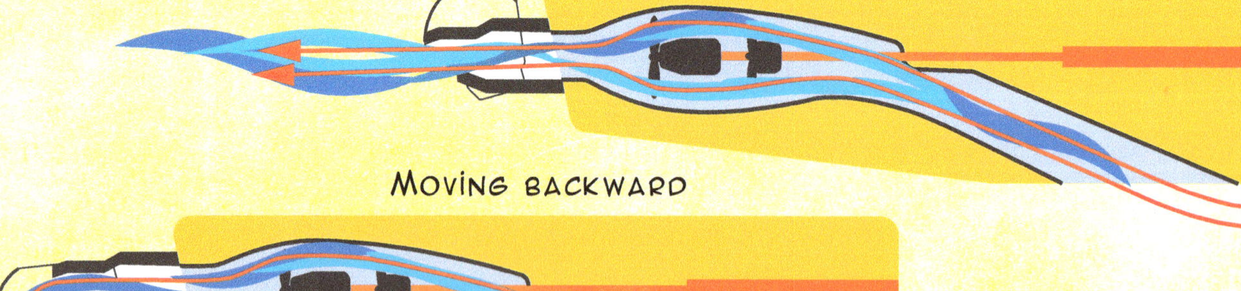

A water jet propulsion unit is like an underwater pump. It sucks water in and then ejects it out with a great power putting the watercraft in motion. The water movement is provided by the propeller rotation.

HOW DEEP HAVE WE GONE?

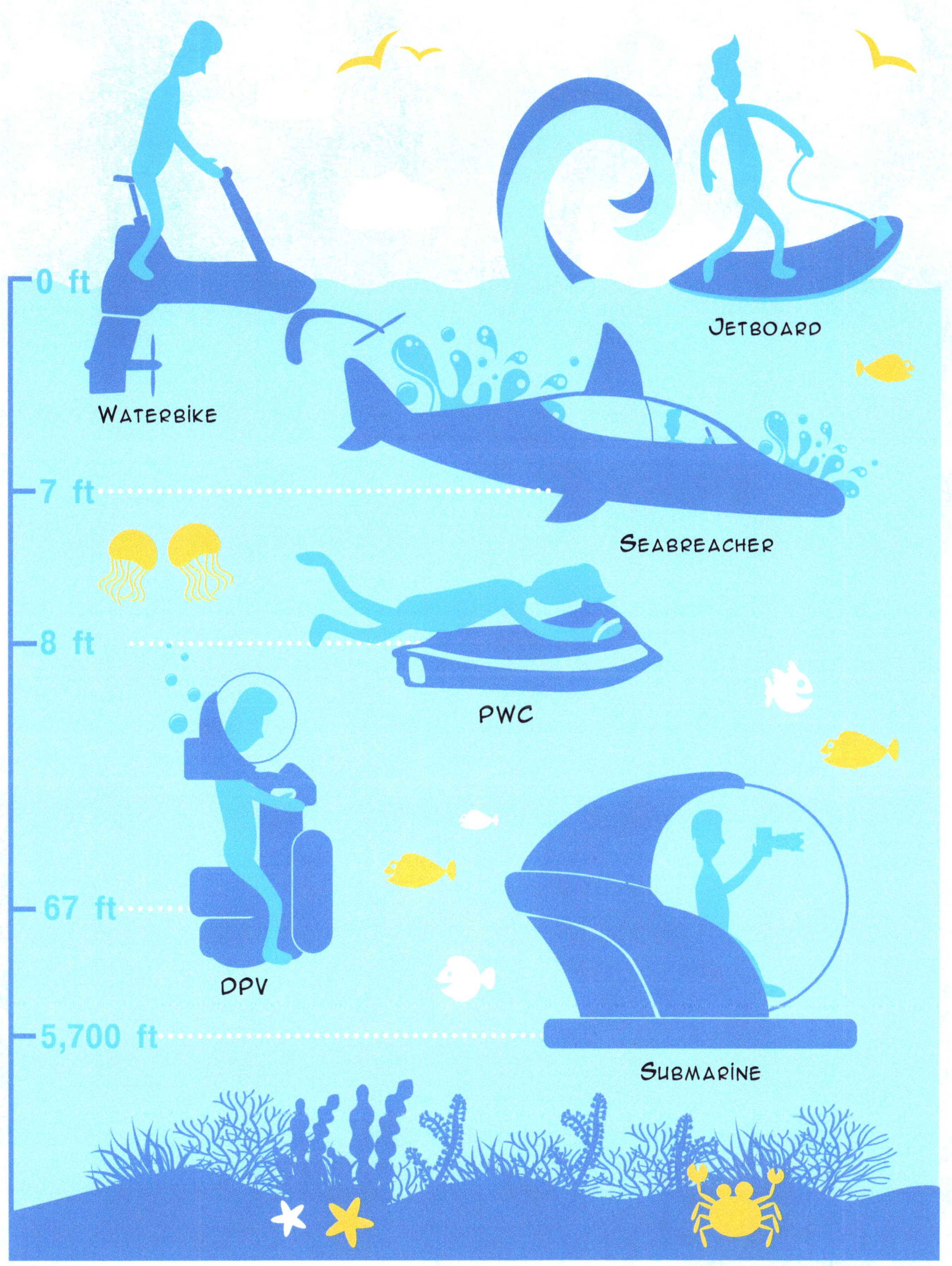

JET PACKS

JET PACK

A person flying in the sky at the speed of a plane is not fiction but a reality of today. Like comics superheroes, they own… a jet pack! The jet pack is a kind of aircraft that is attached to the pilot's back. The first packs functioned due to the mechanical propeller driver. But the greatest popularity is enjoyed by jet driver models

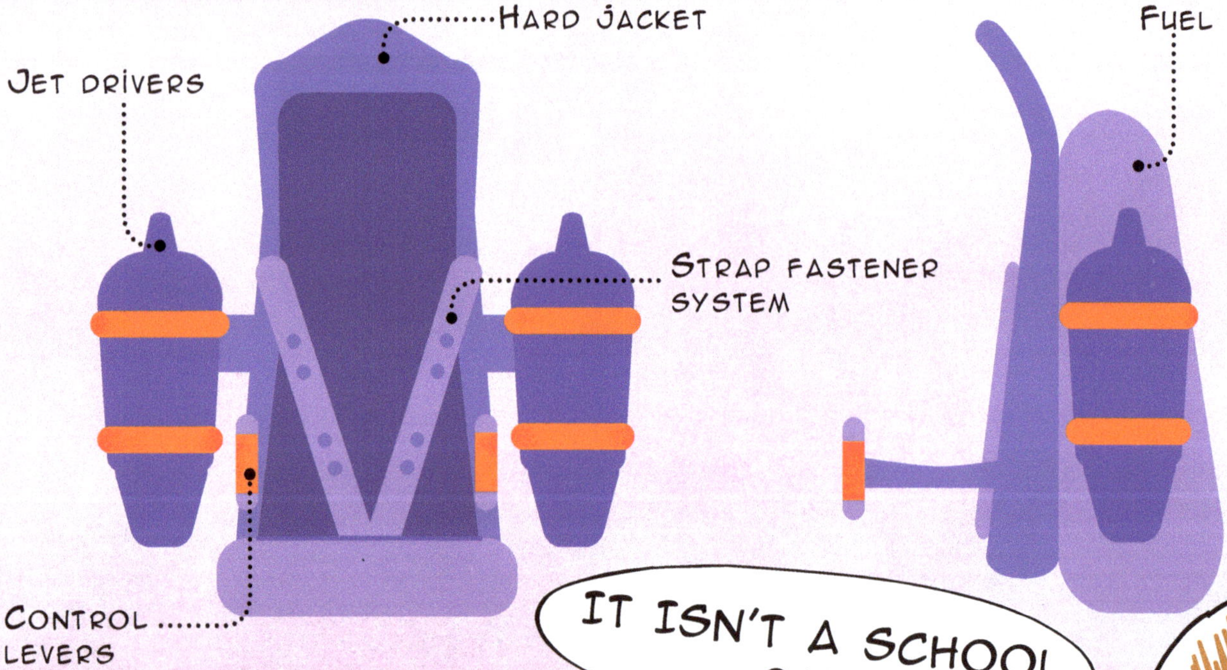

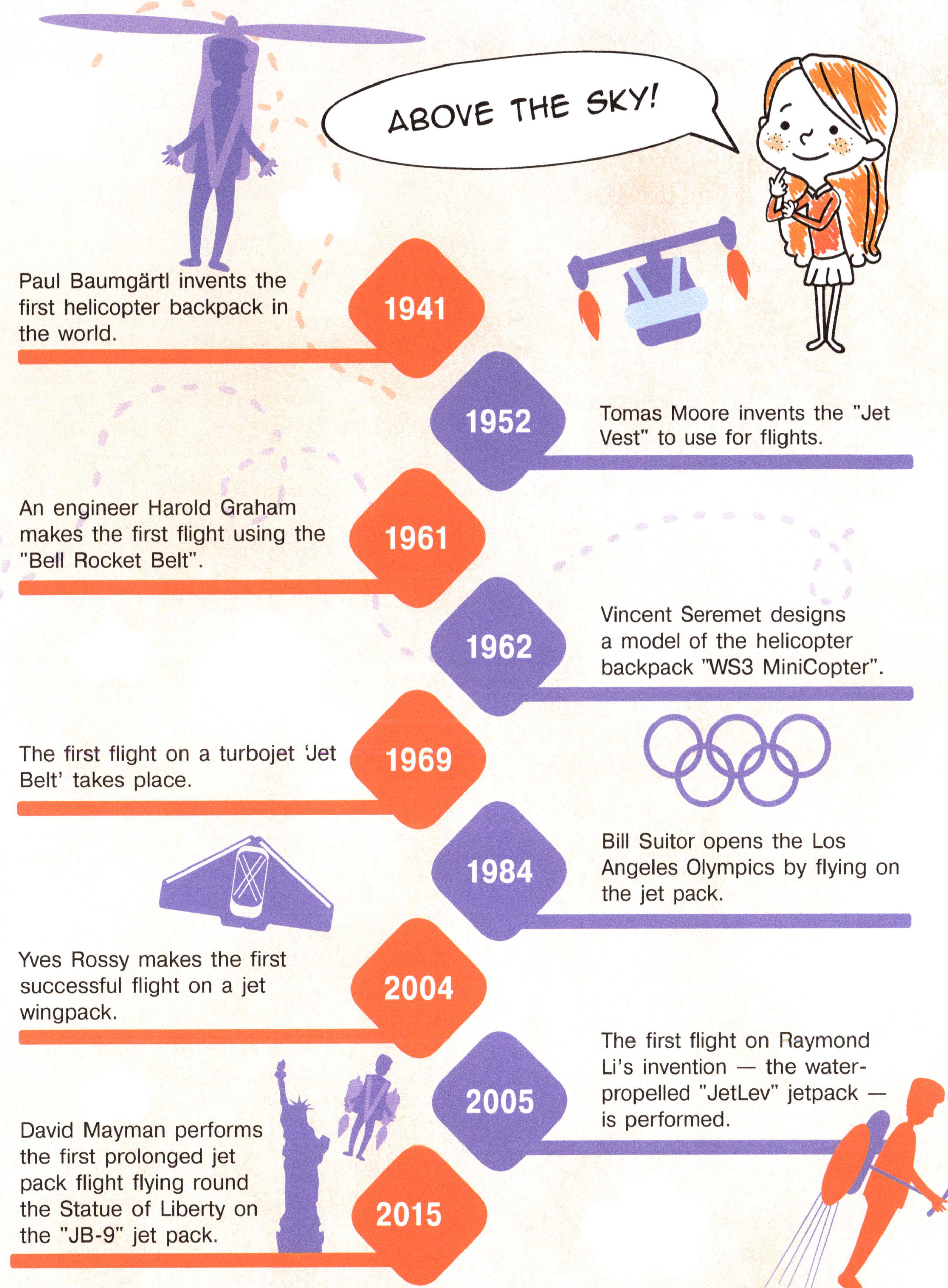

Paul Baumgärtl invents the first helicopter backpack in the world.

1941

1952 Tomas Moore invents the "Jet Vest" to use for flights.

An engineer Harold Graham makes the first flight using the "Bell Rocket Belt".

1961

1962 Vincent Seremet designs a model of the helicopter backpack "WS3 MiniCopter".

The first flight on a turbojet 'Jet Belt' takes place.

1969

1984 Bill Suitor opens the Los Angeles Olympics by flying on the jet pack.

Yves Rossy makes the first successful flight on a jet wingpack.

2004

2005 The first flight on Raymond Li's invention — the water-propelled "JetLev" jetpack — is performed.

David Mayman performs the first prolonged jet pack flight flying round the Statue of Liberty on the "JB-9" jet pack.

2015

JET PACKS

SPECIAL BACKPACKS HAVE BEEN USED IN SPACE FOR A LONG TIME

Inspired by Iron Man movies, Richard Browning and the team of enthusiasts start their work on designing a jet flight pack "Daedalus Mk I", in which jet drivers will be attached to hands and feet.

The jet pack technology is widely used by the main characters of well-known cartoons, sci-fi movies, and even computer games!

JET PACKS CAN FLY AS HIGH AS
15,000 ft
AND AS FAST AS 200 MPH

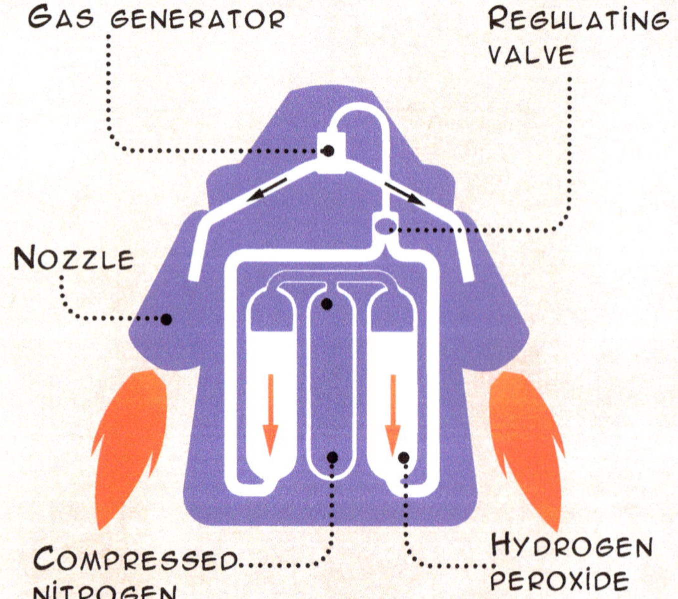

HERE'S HOW THIS WORKS
The compressed nitrogen at high pressure supplants the hydrogen peroxide. It comes to the gas generator where a range of chemical reactions takes place, which results in producing heat and a great amount of gas. The gas comes out of the nozzle and lifts the pilot.

FLYING IS EASY!

Chemical processes are followed by excessive heat outcome, so the pilot needs to wear a protective suit to prevent burns. The jet pack fuel margin is fairly small. The pilot's helmet contains a signaling device which informs the pilot when it is time to land.